Union Public Library

D1456108

WORLD IN FOCUS

FOCUS ON
Japan

CELIA TIDMARSH

Union Public Library

WORLD ALMANAC® LIBRARY

Please visit our web site at: **www.worldalmanaclibrary.com**
**For a free color catalog describing World Almanac® Library's list of high-quality books
and multimedia programs, call 1-800-848-2928 (USA) or 1-800-387-3178 (Canada).
World Almanac® Library's fax: (414) 332-3567.**

Library of Congress Cataloging-in-Publication Data

Tidmarsh, Celia.
    Focus on Japan / by Celia Tidmarsh.
        p. cm. — (World in focus)
    Includes bibliographical references and index.
    ISBN 0-8368-6722-X (lib. bdg.)
    ISBN 0-8368-6729-7 (softcover)
    1. Japan. I. Title. II. World in focus (Milwaukee, Wis.)
  DS806.T55   2006
  952—dc22   2006001921

✝
915.2
TID
c.1

This North American edition first published in 2007 by
World Almanac® Library
A Member of the WRC Media Family of Companies
330 West Olive Street, Suite 100
Milwaukee, WI 53212 USA

This U.S. edition copyright © 2007 by World Almanac® Library. Original edition copyright
© 2005 by Hodder Wayland. First published in 2005 by Hodder Wayland, an imprint of Hodder
Children's Books, a division of Hodder Headline Limited, 338 Euston Road,
London NW1 3BH, U.K.

Commissioning editor: Nicola Edwards
Editor: Patience Coster
Inside design: Chris Halls, www.mindseyedesign.co.uk
Cover design: Wayland
Series concept and project management by EASI-Educational Resourcing (info@easi-er.co.uk)
Statistical research: Anna Bowden
Maps and graphs: Martin Darlison, Encompass Graphics

World Almanac® Library editor: Alan Wachtel
World Almanac® Library cover design: Scott Krall

Population Density Map © 2003 UT-Battelle, LLC. All rights reserved.
Data for population density maps reproduced under licence from UT-Battelle, LLC.
All rights reserved.

Picture acknowledgements:
The author and publisher would like to thank the following for allowing their pictures to be
reproduced in this publication: Corbis 4 and *cover top* (Jose Fuste Raga), 6 (Robert Essel NYC), 9 (Asian
Art & Archaeology Inc.), 12 (Eriko Sugita/Reuters), 13 (Bettmann), 14 (Michael S. Yamashita), 15
(Wolfgang Kaehler), 16 (Michael S. Yamashita), 17 (Issei Kato/Reuters), 23 (Issei Kato/Reuters), 28
(Michael S. Yamashita), 32 (Steve Raymer), 33 (Kimimasa Mayama/Reuters), 37 (Stephane Reix/Photo
& Co.), 44 (Richard T. Nowitz), 45 (Tom Wagner), 52 (Roger Ressmeyer), 54 (Michael S. Yamashita),
57 (Joel W. Rogers), 58 (Photowood Inc.); EASI-Images/Rob Bowden 5, 8, 10 and *title page*, 11, 18, 19,
20, 21, 22, 24, 25, 26, 27, 29, 30, 31, 34, 35, 36, 38, 39, 40, 41, 42, 43, 46, 47, 48, 49 and *cover bottom*, 50,
51, 53, 55, 56, 59.

The directional arrow portrayed on the map on page 7 provides only an approximation of north.
The data used to produce the graphics and data panels in this title were the latest available at
the time of production.

All rights reserved. No part of this book may be reproduced, stored in a retrieval system,
or transmitted in any form or by any means, electronic, mechanical, photocopying,
recording, or otherwise, without the prior written permission of the copyright holder.

Printed in China

1 2 3 4 5 6 7 8 9 10 09 08 07 06

CONTENTS

Cover: A Kabuki theater performance.

Title page: The Meiji shrine, located in Tokyo was built in memory of Emperor Meiji and Empress Shoken. It was completed in 1920.

CHAPTER 1

Japan – An Overview

The country of Japan lies off the eastern coast of the Asian landmass. It is an archipelago of more than 6,800 islands, with the four islands of Hokkaido, Honshu, Shikoku, and Kyushu making up 98 percent of the total land area. The country's land surface area is 144,651 square miles (374,744 square kilometers), slightly smaller than the state of California. Japan is called Nippon (or Nihon) in Japanese, meaning "the source of the sun."

Japan is a rugged country. Over 75 percent of its land area is mountainous or hilly. In the past, the country's diversity of climatic types and habitats supported a rich variety of wildlife, but many species have been lost because of urbanization, deforestation, and overfishing.

Japan lies in one of world's most seismically active regions and is prone to earthquakes. It has 77 active and many dormant volcanoes, including Mount Fuji, which, at 12,389 feet (3,776 meters), is the highest mountain in Japan.

PEOPLE AND HISTORY

Less than 2 percent of Japan's population is from ethnic groups other than Japanese. Settlements in the country are concentrated in the flatter coastal plains, and these regions have some of the highest population densities in the world.

▼ Mount Fuji is a perfect conical volcano. It is one of Japan's most popular attractions and has become a symbol the country.

Most of Japan's population lives in urban areas. The country has twelve cities with more than one million people each. Together, these people make up 21 percent of Japan's population. With more than 8 million people in its central districts and more than 35 million in the wider urban area, Tokyo is Japan's largest city.

Historically, Japan has experienced periods of contact with the outside world and periods of isolation from it. The influence of China dates from the fourth century and has effected language, religion, and architectural styles. Contact with the West began in the 1500s, when trade links were developed, particularly with Portugal, the Netherlands, and Britain. In 1639, however, Tokugawa Iemitsu, a shogun, imposed isolation that was maintained for more than two hundred years. Renewed contact with the West in the mid-1800s led to the adoption of many Western institutions in the fields of law, government, and the military, helping to transform the Empire of Japan into a world power. Following this, several decades of Japanese expansion into neighboring parts of Asia—China and Korea, especially—led to military conflicts with China and Russia between 1894 and 1905. In the twentieth century, expansionism also led to Japan's involvement in two world wars.

ECONOMIC SUCCESS

Between the 1960s and 1980s, Japan experienced remarkable economic growth in spite of its lack of raw materials and the legacy of industrial destruction from World War II. Japan's factories had been bombed by the Allied forces during the war, but its hard-working and highly skilled workforce had helped bring about an extraordinary economic recovery. In spite a decade of recession during the 1990s,

Japan has the second largest economy in the world and is home to many of the world's most successful companies, including Mitsubishi, Sony, Toyota, and Canon. Such companies produce a range of high-tech goods—including personal computers, cars, mobile phones, game consoles, cameras, and music players—that have helped to shape the lifestyles of people in many countries.

 Did You Know?

Tokyo is often cited as the largest city in the world, with a population of over 35 million, but this figure actually refers to Tokyo's metropolitan area, which includes the adjoining prefectures, or political districts, of Chiba, Saitama, and Kanagawa.

▼ The Shinjuku district of Tokyo is a prime example of Japan's economic success. Its busy neon-lit center comes alive in the evening, as people shop and dine on their way home.

◀ In Japan's rural areas, some lifestyles have changed little in hundreds of years. Farming is still important in these areas, and rice is a major crop. Here, rice is being dried near Wakayama, on Honshu.

ENVIRONMENTAL CHALLENGES

Japan's rapid pace of industrialization and the size of its population have created environmental challenges, including overcrowding and pollution. Japan has developed a range of strategies to cope with the increasing spread of urban and industrial areas. These strategies include the reclamation of land from the sea. Extensive pollution has caused considerable damage to human health and to the environment. Pollution problems are being tackled with some success, but problems such as the disposal of nuclear waste and dioxins continue to cause concern.

CULTURE AND POLITICS

Japan is a modern and economically developed society, but it also maintains many cultural traditions, including the celebration of long-established festivals such as *O-bon* in August. Contemporary cultural interests include reading *manga* (comic strips) and watching *animes* (animated feature films and TV shows), both of which are produced in Japan.

As a member of the G8 (a group of the eight wealthiest nations in the world), Japan occupies a powerful position in global politics. Also, its relations with countries such as China, South Korea and North Korea are vital to the stability of South-east Asia.

Physical Geography

▱ Land area: 144,651 sq miles/374,744 sq km

▱ Water area: 1,193 sq miles/3,091 sq km

▱ Total area: 145,844 sq miles/377,835 sq km

▱ World rank (by area): 61

▱ Land boundaries: 0 miles/0 km

▱ Border countries: none

▱ Coastline: 18,487 miles/29,751 km

▱ Highest point: Mount Fuji (12,389 ft/ 3,776 m)

▱ Lowest point: Hachiro-Gata (-13 ft/-4 m)

Source: CIA World Factbook

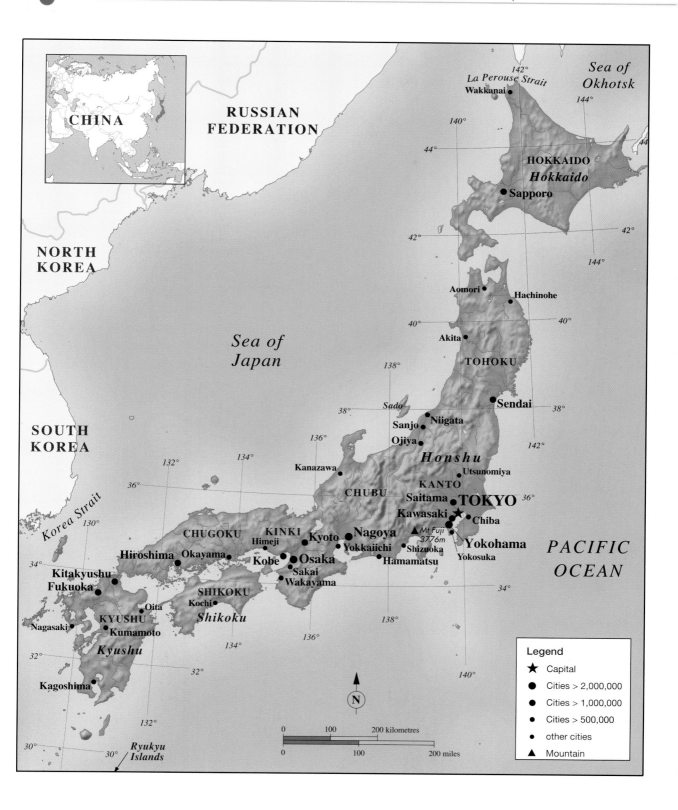

CHINA

RUSSIAN
FEDERATION

*Sea of
Okhotsk*

La Perouse Strait
Wakkanai ●

142°

144°

140°

44°

44

HOKKAIDO
Hokkaido

● Sapporo

42°

42°

144°

NORTH
KOREA

Aomori ●

● Hachinohe

40°

40°

Akita ●

*Sea of
Japan*

138°

TOHOKU

SOUTH
KOREA

38°   Sado

● Sendai

38°

142°

Sanjo ●   ● Niigata

Ojiya ●

Honshu

136°

Kanazawa ●

Utsunomiya ●

132°   134°

36°

CHUBU

KANTO
Saitama ●   ★ **TOKYO**   36°

Kawasaki ●

CHUGOKU

KINKI

Kyoto ●   **Nagoya** ●

▲ *Mt Fuji
3776m*

● Chiba

130°

Himeji ●

Yokkaiichi ●

Shizuoka ●

Yokohama

*PACIFIC
OCEAN*

Hiroshima ●   Okayama ●

Kobe ●   ● **Osaka**

Hamamatsu ●

Yokosuka ●

34°

Kitakyushu ●
Fukuoka ●

Sakai ●
Wakayama ●

34°

SHIKOKU

Oita ●   Kochi ●

Shikoku

138°

Nagasaki ●   **KYUSHU**

32°   Kumamoto ●

Kyushu

136°

134°

32°

Kagoshima ●

132°

140°

30°

*Ryukyu
Islands*   30°

N

0   100   200 kilometres

0   100   200 miles

Korea Strait

Legend

★ Capital

● Cities > 2,000,000

● Cities > 1,000,000

● Cities > 500,000

• other cities

▲ Mountain

CHAPTER 2

History

Signs of early settlement in what is now Japan can be traced back 30,000 years. It is believed that, at that time, Japan was joined to the Asian mainland by two land bridges, one to the north and one to the south. The earliest inhabitants probably migrated over these land bridges and were probably hunter-gatherers who used stone tools and weapons. Beginning in about 10,000 B.C., humans developed skills in pottery that allowed for improvements in the cooking and storing of food. The importance of these developments is reflected in the fact that the era between 10,000 B.C. and 300 B.C. is called the Jomon period—named after the style of decoration on pottery made during that time.

CHINESE INFLUENCES

From 300 B.C. to A.D. 300, during the period known as Yayoi, Japan was heavily influenced by ideas brought by migrants from China. These included the growing of rice as a staple crop, the working of iron, and the weaving of cloth. Between the fourth and the seventh centuries, contact with China increased further, and Japan adopted many aspects of Chinese culture, including its writing system and calendar. Chinese technologies for making porcelain, silk, and paper were also introduced. Buddhism also came to Japan from China. Buddhism fitted well with Shinto, a religion already being practiced in Japan, because it offered teachings on death while Shinto focused on life in this world.

SHOGUNS AND FEUDAL RULE

By the seventh century, Japan was ruled as an empire, although some historians think that Japan's line of emperors can be traced back to

 Did You Know?

The Ainu were one of the earliest peoples to inhabit Japan. They are believed to have come originally from Siberia, because they share some skeletal characteristics with peoples from that area. On the island of Hokkaido, there are still some Ainu who speak a language quite different from Japanese.

◀ Calligraphy, known as *sho*, was brought to Japan in the seventh century by Buddhist monks who used Chinese calligraphy in their scriptures.

A.D. 400, when a powerful family, the Fugiwara clan, controlled central Honshu. From the seventh to the eleventh centuries, the imperial court of the emperor was at its peak of power and influence in terms of the size of the territory it covered. The emperor had absolute power and was considered to be divinely appointed as a living god. This period is named the Heian (meaning "peace" in Japanese) era and was noted for its art, poetry, and literature. By the end of this era in the twelfth century, however, military leaders, or shoguns, had become very powerful. In 1192, Minamoto Yoritomo became the first shogun to seize control of government from the imperial court. Several centuries dominated by military rule followed, with leaders of different powerful families often battling for the title of shogun.

The Edo era (1600–1868) was dominated by the last shogun family, the Tokugawa clan. In 1603, the Tokugawa leader Ieyasu emerged as the most powerful feudal lord. He built a new capital at Edo (present day Tokyo). Everyday life for most Japanese people was grim and tightly controlled through a rigid feudal system in which a strict social hierarchy was imposed. The shogun were at the top, followed by the samurai and commoners.

▲ An illustration from 1865 shows soldiers forcing commoners to kneel before the shogun as he approaches on a journey from Edo (now Tokyo) to Kyoto to meet with the emperor.

Focus on: The Seclusion of Japan during the Edo Era

The isolationist policies of Edo-era Japan included banning Christianity, expelling foreigners, and ending almost all overseas trade. Japanese people were also forbidden to leave the islands of Japan. For commercial reasons, people from China and the Dutch East India Company were allowed to visit Japan, but they were restricted to the island of Dejima, near the port of Nagasaki. Any foreigners landing elsewhere in Japan were sentenced to death. After 1853, relations with foreign countries were re-established when a fleet from the United States, led by Commodore Perry, sailed to Japan and demanded that it "open up" to trade. In economic terms, many people in Japan benefitted from this opening. The shogun rulers, however, were weakened by it, and their reign ended in 1868.

The Edo era also saw the development of cultural rituals, some of which, such as the Japanese tea ceremony, still exist today. The rituals were elaborate and expensive, and they took up time and money that might otherwise have been used to mount a rebellion against the rulers. The rituals, therefore, helped the Tokugawa family control the other clans. In 1639, Japan was cut off from external influences when isolationist policies were imposed by Iemitsu, a later Tokugawa shogun.

MODERNIZATION, IMPERIALISM, AND WAR

Between 1868 and 1912, the Meiji era (Meiji means "enlightened rule") saw the resignation of the last Tokugawa shogun, Yoshinobu.

▼ The Meiji shrine, located in Tokyo was built in memory of Emperor Meiji and Empress Shoken. It was completed in 1920.

Following the Boshin War (1868–1869) between Yoshinobu and pro-imperial forces, the emperor was re-established as the country's ruler, and Japan became known as the Empire of Japan. The emperor continued to be advised by leaders of the pro-imperial forces, such as Okubo Toshimichi and Saigo Takamori, who had a great influence on how Japan was governed. They were behind decisions such as the lifting of restrictions on contact with foreign

 Did You Know?

During the rule of the shoguns, the samurai—the warriors of the lords—were the only people, apart from the shoguns, who were allowed be armed. The samurai had the legal right to kill any commoners—such as peasants, artisans, merchants, outcasts, and others in the social classes below them—who did not show respect for their feudal lord.

peoples, which allowed trade with Europe and China to develop again. Japan began to modernize, bringing in foreign experts to teach in specialized fields such as engineering and science. Feudalism was abolished and the principle of democratic government was established, although only wealthy men over the age of 25 were allowed to vote.

Japan needed raw materials to fuel its rapid industrialization so it set out to annex neighboring territories. The first Sino-Japanese War (1894–1895) was fought in Korea, and led to Japan's annexation of Taiwan (then called Formosa). The Russo-Japanese War (1904–1905) was fought in Manchuria and led to Japan's annexation of Korea.

During World War I (1914–1918), Japan fought on the side of the Allies and emerged in 1919 as a major world power, with increased influence in Asia. After the war, a democratic system of government was re-established. During the early 1920s, however, economic problems made worse in the Tokyo area by the devastation caused by the Great Kanto earthquake in 1923 led to a rise in the influence of military leaders. Extreme nationalism, focusing on the preservation of traditional Japanese values and the rejection of Western influence, took hold and became increasingly popular. In 1931, nationalist extremists assassinated the Japanese prime minister, Hamaguchi Osachi, and military leaders gained influence. Japan again undertook military action to expand its territory. Japanese forces invaded Manchuria in 1931. In 1937, the country launched into a second major war against China that developed into the Pacific War and became part of World War II (1939–1945). The Imperial Japanese Army carried out widespread atrocities during the

war with China. These atrocities included the 1937 Massacre of Nanjing, in which over 300,000 unarmed civilians of the city of Nanjing are alleged to have been killed.

▲ Osaka Castle is one of several fine castles in Japan. It was first completed in 1583 but has been rebuilt several times, most recently in 1931.

DEFEAT AND OCCUPATION

In 1940, the fall of France to Japan's ally, Germany, led to the Japan's occupation of French Indochina. On December 7, 1941, Japan launched a surprise attack on the United States naval base at Pearl Harbor in which more than 2,500 U.S. sailors were killed. The United States responded by declaring war on Japan. In 1942, Japan seized control of Singapore and the Philippines. But Japan lost battles to the Allies, including the Battle of Midway, and in August 1945, the United States dropped atomic bombs on the cities of Hiroshima and Nagasaki, forcing Japan's rapid surrender. The Allies imposed a new constitution on Japan, and U.S. forces occupied the country for the next seven years. After occupation ended, Japan signed an alliance with the United States that has been maintained in various forms ever since. Japan regained political independence in 1952, although the United States retained the Okinawa islands for military use. In 1972, the islands were transferred back to Japan,

▼ This building in Hiroshima was one of the few left standing after the city was hit by an atomic bomb in 1945. Now known as the A-bomb Dome, it is a permanent memorial to those who died.

 Did You Know?

On March 9, 1945, in just one night of firebombing by the U.S. military, more than 100,000 Japanese, most of them civilians, were killed in Tokyo. Six hundred bombers dropped more than 500,000 incendiary bombs. About 16 square miles (41 sq km) of the city were completely destroyed.

Focus on: The Atomic Bombs of 1945

On August 6, 1945, an American B29 bomber dropped a uranium atomic bomb on the city of Hiroshima. Three days later, a second atomic bomb, this time using plutonium, was dropped on the city of Nagasaki. By the end of 1945, more than 200,000 Japanese had died as a result of these bombings. This total does not include the thousands of Koreans who were working as slave laborers in factories in the two cities. In the years immediately following the bombings, nothing was known in Japan about the nuclear fallout and radiation sickness that went on to kill thousands more. Sixty years after the bombings, people are still dying from cancers caused by nuclear radiation.

although U.S. forces are still based there. Even after the changes in its government, Japan kept an emperor on the Chrysanthemum Throne, the oldest hereditary monarchy in the world. But this emperor has had no ruling powers or influence on the elected government since the end of World War II.

RECOVERY AND GROWTH

During the 1960s and 1970s, rapid growth returned Japan to economic strength, and it became the world's leading manufacturer of ships and steel. During the 1970s, oil crises caused the Japanese government to rethink its whole economy. Japan's heavy industries used large quantities of oil, of which Japan had none of its own supplies. This made Japan dependent on other countries for vital supplies of energy. To remedy this problem, Japan began a nuclear energy program and started to switch from heavy industries to higher value and high-tech industries producing goods such as cameras and electronics. Japan soon became famous worldwide for efficiency and advanced technology.

INTO THE TWENTY-FIRST CENTURY

In the 1990s, Japan faced growing economic competition from the "Asian Tigers." The slump in economic growth that occurred during this time has become known as Japan's "lost decade." The country's economy improved in the early twenty-first century. Some significant political changes also took place. The dominant political party, the Liberal Democratic Party (LDP), suffered a temporary loss of power in 1993, as a result of political scandals and corruption involving some of its politicians. Eventually the LDP regained power in 2000. Its popularity

▲ A production line making Sony Trinitron televisions in 1973. The manufacturing of electronic goods was a major factor in Japan's economic recovery during the 1960s and 1970s.

increased again following the election in 2001 of Junichiro Koizumi as prime minister. Koizumi's flamboyant personality made him popular with the people, as did his assurances that he would deal with economic problems and corruption. Koizumi has spearheaded considerable developments in Japan's foreign policy. In 2002, for example, he became the first Japanese prime minister to visit the communist state of North Korea.

CHAPTER 3

Landscape and Climate

J apan is made up of about 6,800 islands that form a crescent-shaped archipelago lying north to south. It stretches over more than 20 degrees of latitude, is located in the Pacific Ocean, and is separated from the east coast of Asia by the Sea of Japan. Japan's nearest neighbors are Russia, to the northwest; North and South Korea, to the west; and China, to the southwest. The nearest country on the Asian mainland is South Korea, at a distance of approximately 124 miles (200 km) over the Korea Strait.

MOUNTAINS, RIVERS, LAKES, AND COASTS

While Mount Fuji is Japan's highest mountain, the country has fourteen other peaks over 9,843 ft (3,000 m). Most of these are extinct or dormant volcanoes and are part of the Japanese Alps that run through central Honshu. The low-lying areas

▼ The coastline near Kagoshima on Kyushu is very rocky. These formations are the result of volcanic activity that forced lava up through the sea.

of Japan are broken up into many small plains, separated from one another by high ground. The largest lowland area is the Kanto Plain on Honshu. It is about 5,018 sq miles (13,000 sq km) in area and is the location of Japan's largest urban area, including the city of Tokyo.

Japan's rivers drain either to the east into the Pacific Ocean or to the west into the Sea of Japan, which is located between between Japan and Korea. The country's rivers are very short and nowhere in Japan is far from the sea. The longest river is the Shinano, which flows over 228 miles (367 km) through the Nagano and Niigata prefectures into the Sea of Japan. Rivers in the mountains are fast-flowing and provide considerable potential for the generation of hydroelectric power (HEP). At certain times year, when rainfall or snowfall is high, there is a significant risk of flooding in the lower reaches of these rivers. To reduce this risk, concrete channels have been built to channel water quickly and efficiently into the sea.

There are many lakes in Japan's uplands, often in the craters of old volcanoes. The largest of these is Lake Biwa, which measures 259 sq miles (670 sq km). The next in size is Lake Kasumi, measuring 65 sq miles (168 sq km). Lake Biwa is famous for its beauty and is a popular place for leisure pursuits. During the 1980s, it was polluted with sewage and urban waste, but it was cleaned up in the late 1990s.

As an archipelago, Japan has a very long coastline of 18,487 miles (29,751 kilometers). The Pacific coastline to the south of Tokyo has many long, narrow, and relatively shallow inlets that provide natural harbors. The Inland Sea separates the islands of Shikoku, Honshu, and Kyushu.

▲ Lake Mashu in Akan National Park, on Hokkaido, is often called Japan's most beautiful lake. Its waters are clear to a depth of up to 115 ft (35 m).

 A man pushes his bicycle past one of the many thousands of homes destroyed in the Kobe earthquake of 1995. This earthquake killed more than 6,000 people in Japan.

VOLCANOES AND EARTHQUAKES

Japan is located on the very unstable part of Earth's crust where three tectonic plates— the Pacific, Philippine, and Eurasian—meet. Movement of the plates causes volcanoes and earthquakes. As a consequence of its location, Japan has about 10 percent of the world's active volcanoes. Volcanoes that have erupted in the last ten years include Tokachi, on Hokkaido; Aso, on Kyushu; and Asama, Honshu's most active volcano, located 87 miles (140 km) northwest of Tokyo.

Earthquakes are frequent in Japan, with as many as 1,500 recorded per year. Most of these are minor tremors. Major earthquakes that cause considerable damage and loss of life are very infrequent. In October 2004, an earthquake measuring 6.2 on the Richter scale struck the town of Ojiya and its surrounding area in the Niigata prefecture. More than twenty people were killed, 1,800 were injured, and 60,000 were evacuated from their homes. Earthquakes of this scale often cause other hazards, such as landslides and tsunamis.

Did You Know?

Although Mount Fuji is now dormant, it used to be an active volcano. Between the years of 781 and 1707, it erupted at least sixteen times. It has not erupted since 1707.

EFFECTS OF LATITUDE

Japan lies almost directly north to south, which means that latitude is a major influence on its climate. Hokkaido, to the country's north, has cool summers and long, cold winters during which average temperatures often fall below freezing. In contrast, Kyushu, to the south, has a humid, subtropical climate with winter temperatures generally above 50° F (10° C). Japan also experiences seasonal variations, particularly in precipitation. Average annual precipitation is about 79 inches (2,000 millimeters). Approximately 75 percent of this falls between June and October because the prevailing winds that blow in from the warm Pacific Ocean are laden with moisture during this time. These conditions can create typhoons that bring torrential rains and strong winds, causing damage and disruption. In the winter months, prevailing winds from the Asian landmass often bring heavy snow to the north and northwest of Japan. The snow blocks roads and causes flooding when it melts.

▼ Residents rescue possessions from flooded houses in Sanjo, about 186 miles (300 km) north of Tokyo, following a typhoon in July 2004 that caused widespread damage.

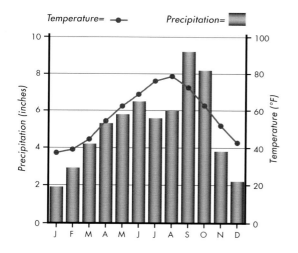

▲ Average monthly climate conditions in Tokyo

Focus on: Typhoons

Japan lies in the path of severe storms that originate in tropical areas of the Pacific Ocean where sea temperatures are above 81° F (27° C). These storms, known in Japan as typhoons, occur between the months of July and October when sea temperatures are high. Typhoons with winds of between 78 and 155 miles per hour (125–249 kilometers per hour) and torrential rains may cause loss of life and great damage. In October 2004, more than seventy people died, hillsides were washed away, and trees were uprooted during Typhoon Tokage, the most destructive typhoon to hit Japan in twenty-five years.

CHAPTER 4

Population and Settlements

The population of Japan is about 127.8 million. Until the mid-1980s, Japan's population experienced significant growth, rising from 99 million in 1965 to 121 million in 1985. Since then, this growth has slowed, and the birth rate has fallen from 1,948 per 1,000 in 1975 to 1,139 per 1,000 in 2003. Projections indicate that Japan's population will fall to about 124 million by 2020. One reason for this decrease is that the age at which Japanese men and women marry has risen from 28.9 years for men and 24.2 years for women in 1970 to 29.4 and 27.6, respectively, in 2003. It seems that women are delaying getting married because it often means they can no longer work outside the home. In traditional Japanese culture, married women are seen as homemakers.

LIFE EXPECTANCY

As Japan's birth rate has fallen, life expectancy in the country has increased from 73 years, in 1975, to 83 years, in 2003. This combination of trends is leading to an ageing of the population. The proportion of people in Japan over the age of 65 has increased from 8 percent in 1975 to 19 percent in 2003, while the proportion of those under the age of 15 has fallen from 25 percent to 14 percent over the same period. By 2020, the proportion of people in Japan over age 65 is expected to be about 27 percent.

These trends, which are common to many developed countries, are viewed with concern by Japan's government. It fears that a growing proportion of older people will put a strain on the country's health and pension services. A more positive view suggests that, in wealthy countries such as Japan, people remain youthful because of healthy lifestyles and high quality health care. They, therefore, have the potential to earn their own livings for longer than in the past. Japan already has a tradition of people, although usually only men, staying economically active into their 70s and 80s.

◀ Kogan-ji Temple in Sugamo, Tokyo, is popular with some older people. These people believe that if they pour water over a small statue called Migawari Kannon, it will take away their aches, pains, and other medical problems.

ETHNIC ORIGINS

Over 98 percent of Japan's population is ethnically Japanese, making it one of the most homogenous countries in the world. This is partly because few people migrated to Japan before the twentieth century. In the early twentieth century, however, Japan's occupation of Korea and Taiwan resulted in people from these countries migrating to work in Japan's coal mines. Today, approximately 0.6 percent of the population is Korean, and many of these people are descendants of the earlier miners. (Citizenship in Japan is based on nationality of parents, not place of birth.)

Two other groups are identified as different from mainstream Japanese society: the Ainu and the *buraku*. The Ainu are an indigenous minority group with a distinctive culture. The present-day Ainu are descended from hunter-gatherers who settled in the northern Japanese islands before 300 B.C. The Ainu are dwindling in numbers and are now only found living on Hokkaido. They have suffered from discrimination in the past, and although there is now greater recognition of their rights and culture, they are often seen by mainstream Japanese society only as a tourist attraction. The *buraku* people, another minority group, also face discrimination.

▲ A busy pedestrian crossing in Osaka's city center. Although Japan has a large population, most of its people are from a single ethnic group.

 Did You Know?

It is rare in Japan for unmarried couples to have children. The rising age at which women in Japan are marrying has caused the age at which a typical Japanese mother has her first child to rise from 25.6, in 1970, to 28.6, in 2003.

Population Data

- Population: 127.8 million
- Population 0–14 yrs: 14%
- Population 15–64 yrs: 67%
- Population 65+ yrs: 19%
- Population growth rate: 0.1%
- Population density: 883.3 per sq mile/ 341.0 per sq km
- Urban population: 65%
- Major cities: Tokyo 35,327,000
  Osaka 11,286,000
  Nagoya 3,189,000

Source: United Nations and World Bank

WHERE PEOPLE LIVE

Japan's population is very unevenly distributed because of the limited amount of flat, low land suitable for settlements and the fast rate at which urbanization has taken place. The average population density for Japan as a whole is 883.3 people per sq mile (341 per sq km). Some regions are sparsely populated; Hokkaido, for example, has 189 people per sq mile (73 per sq km). But some Tokyo districts have about 28,490 people per sq mile (11,000 people per sq km), one of the highest population densities in the world.

▲ The level land around Lake Biwa is densely settled. Most land in this area is mountainous. Level land in Japan is very valuable.

Approximately 65 percent of Japan's people live in urban areas. The rate of urbanization has been very high during the past fifty years, with rural areas losing people to the fast-growing towns and cities. Since the 1970s much of Japan's urban growth has come from an internal population increase, and small town and rural populations have stabilized. Of Japan's twelve cities with more than one million people each, all but one (Sapporo) are located in the Pacific Belt on the Kanto Plain, on Honshu. At the eastern end of the Pacific Belt, the major cities of Tokyo, Yokohama, Kawasaki, and Chiba have spread and joined to make a metropolitan area containing 35 million people.

INSIDE CITIES

Japanese cities do not have the rich and poor districts or neighborhoods commonly found in the cities of the United States and Britain, where many poor people live in run-down inner-city areas with social problems, while the wealthy live in well-maintained suburbs. It is often thought that this is because Japanese society is more equal than elsewhere. Although Japan does have less of a gap between the incomes of rich and poor than Britain and the United States, significant differences still exist between households. These differences are reflected in income, job status, and quality of housing. However, "well-off" and "less well-off" households are not generally concentrated in particular areas of Japan's cities (although

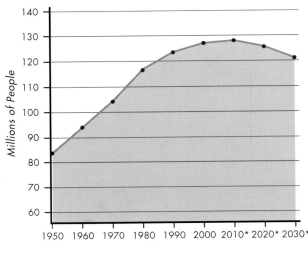

* Projected Population

▲ Population growth 1950–2030

there are exceptions). Part of the reason for this is that Japanese employers usually pay the transportation costs of their employees, so poorer people can live in the suburbs and commute to work. Also, wealthy residents do not usually express their social status through where they live. This is because, in Japan, people who want to impress friends or work colleagues tend to take them out to restaurants rather than entertain them at home.

▲ High-density housing is the only practical and affordable option in Japan's main cities, where space is very limited.

Focus on: The *Buraku* People

Although ethnically identical to other Japanese people, the *buraku* people, or *burakumin*, are discriminated against because they are descendants of an outcast class that existed in the feudal system of the seventeenth century. During that time, the *burakumin* were at the bottom of a rigid hierarchy, doing jobs that were associated with the impurities of death, such as burials. Within the Buddhist and Shinto religions, they were thought to be polluted. This caste system was abolished in 1871, and today, the *burakumin* are no longer required to wear special clothes and live separately. Some, however, still live in *burakumin* communities that are generally looked down upon by the wider society. They still face discrimination, particularly when they wish to marry or apply for a job. Potential

marriage partners or employers can find out the details of an individual's origins through Japan's family registry system. If the person's origins are *burakumin*, there is a strong possibility that he or she will be rejected. This discrimination leads to unhappiness and economic problems. A recent survey by the Buraku Liberation League (BLL), an organization that fights for *burakumin* rights, showed that unemployment figures in *burakumin* communities, such as the Kuboyoshi district of Osaka, were twice the national average. Japan has more than 4,000 *burakumin* communities, with an official population total of 892,000. However, the BLL believes the total is higher, at around three million, because many people do not admit publicly to being *burakumin*.

CHAPTER 5

Government and Politics

Japan has a democratic parliamentary government that is based on a constitution. The country's parliament is made up of the House of Representatives and the House of Councillors, known jointly as the Diet. All Japanese citizens over the age of 20, regardless of gender or ethnic origins, are able to vote for members of the Diet. These members elect the prime minister, who is the head of government. The prime minister is usually the leader of the largest political party represented in the Diet.

▼ The National Diet Building in Tokyo is the seat of the Japanese government. It was built between 1920 and 1936 and stands at the center of a district of government buildings located behind the Imperial Palace.

THE LIBERAL DEMOCRATIC PARTY

Since the 1950s, one party, the Liberal Democratic Party, has dominated Japan's political scene. In 1993, the LDP fell from power for the first time in twenty years as a result of political scandals and corruption. Some LDP politicians were accused of "buying" support by setting up schemes that directed public money toward projects that were not necessary but benefited certain groups. For example, roads were built that were not needed but which provided jobs in the construction industry. These schemes were financed by public money from sources such as the savings bank run by the state-owned postal system, Japan Post. Nevertheless, the lack of a

strong opposition party has led to the LDP's recovery in recent years and, in 2000, it became the ruling party again. Since then, support for the LDP has varied. It only held power in the 2003 election by virtue of a coalition with two minor parties, but it won the 2005 election with the biggest majority since the 1980s.

JAPAN'S MONARCHY

Headed by an emperor and known as the Chrysanthemum Throne, Japan has the world's oldest hereditary monarchy. Until World War II, its emperor had the status of a living god, but the new constitution imposed after the war changed this. The emperor now has no political power and answers to the elected government.

THE CONSTITUTION AND FOREIGN POLICY

Japan's present constitution dates from 1947 and provides the foundation for a democratic, peaceful nation. Article 9 of its constitution renounces the use of force to settle international disputes. Until 2003, Japan's foreign policy was strongly pacifist, in line with its constitution. Since World War II, Japan has had Self Defense Forces (SDF) instead of a traditional military. The SDF have been concerned only with defending Japan from a direct attack. In 1992, a law was passed allowing the SDF to venture abroad as long as they were part of a United Nations (UN) mission and that a ceasefire was in place. This enabled Japan to contribute to peace-keeping in a number of countries, including Cambodia, in 1992; Mozambique, in 1993; and East Timor, in 2002. In 2003, however, Prime Minister Koizumi proposed an emergency law to allow the SDF to be sent to Iraq, to show support for the United States. The troops were to be sent to support reconstruction efforts—a

humanitarian rather than an aggressive role— but there was concern among opposition politicians and the public that Japan was moving away from its pacifist principles. The law was passed and, in 2004, for the first time since World War II, Japan's troops were sent to a combat zone.

▲ Japan's prime minister, Junichiro Koizumi (right), at a campaign rally before the 2003 election.

 **Did You Know?**

Although they have been able to vote since 1947, very few women hold positions of power in Japan's government. In 2004, women made up only 9.7 percent of members of the Diet (the national parliament). A government strategy know as the Plan for Gender Equality 2000 has set a target of 30 percent for 2007, but progress toward this goal has been slow.

Other pressures on Japan also have caused it to reconsider its pacifist stance. For example, there are threats from neighboring North Korea, and there has been an increase in international security issues related to terrorism.

INTERNATIONAL RELATIONS

Japan's relations with its neighboring countries— China, Russia, South Korea, and North Korea—are very complex. Japan recognizes the need for cooperation between them, not least because of the high degree of economic interdependence that exists in the region. This has become increasingly important over the past ten years, as the economies of China and South Korea have grown stronger. Japan's standing in the region, however, is considerably hampered by legacies from World War II. Japan has made statements apologizing for its wartime atrocities, but various present-day incidents continue to cause tension. For example, in 2005, Prime Minister Koizumi insisted on carrying out formal visits to the Yasukuni war memorial, which he had visited every year since he was first elected in 2001. This memorial honors some of Japan's military leaders of the past, including those convicted as war criminals for crimes against Chinese and Korean citizens. China and South Korea strongly resented this, not least because they feared that Prime Minister Koizumi might favor a return to Japan's more militaristic past.

▼ The controversial Yasukuni war memorial is at the center of tense diplomatic relations between Japan and its neighbors in China and South Korea.

Since the end of World War II, Japan has maintained a significant and generally positive relationship with the United States. From the end of the war until 1952, the United States occupied Japan. In 1960, the U.S.-Japan Security Treaty was signed, in which it was agreed that the United States would provide Japan with a nuclear shield. According to this treaty, U.S. military vessels equipped with nuclear weapons would patrol Japan's waters and respond to a military attack on Japan. This agreement continues today, providing the United States with an essential strategic base in the Pacific, while Japan benefits from U.S. protection. In recent years, there has been some debate among Japanese politicians about whether Japan should take responsibility for its own defense and not be so closely tied to the United States.

? Did You Know?

Japan has ongoing territorial disputes with all of its neighboring countries that concern several different groups of islands. For example, Japan refuses to accept that the Southern Kuril Islands, known as the "northern territories" in Japan, are part of Russia, as was claimed by Russia at the end of World War II. As a result, Russia and Japan have still not signed a post-war peace treaty.

Focus on: The Future of the Chrysanthemum Throne

The Chrysanthemum Throne gets its name from the chrysanthemum flower that is featured in the coat of arms of Japan's Imperial Household. It is the world's oldest hereditary monarchy and has existed for over 2,600 years. Until World War II, this imperial dynasty ruled Japan, but it was replaced by a democratic government in 1947. Since then, the Imperial Household, headed by the emperor, performs only ceremonial and social duties. The 1889 Imperial House Law regulates succession and forbids women from ascending to the throne. By 2005, however, no boys had been born into the family for nearly forty years. The immediate heir to the throne, Prince Naruhito, has a daughter who was born in 2001. Concern over the continuing of the imperial line, which has been unbroken for 125 generations, prompted Prime Minister Koizumi to set up a special commission of legal experts to discuss whether to reform the law in 2006. There have been eight empresses in Japan's past, the last in the 1700s. Japan's empresses have only reigned until a male heir has grown old enough to take over. According to a recent poll, Japan's people may be ready to accept a change, with 80 percent of them happy for a woman to take the throne.

▲ Nijubashi Bridge and a seventeenth-century guard tower make up part of the Imperial Palace compound, which is located in central Tokyo.

Energy and Resources

Japan is very short on domestic energy resources, with limited oil and natural gas reserves. Because Japan is the fourth largest energy consumer in the world—after the United States, China, and Russia—it must import energy resources to meet demand. Japan is the world's second-largest energy importer, after the United States. Until 1973, Japan relied on cheap oil imports from the Middle East. Following oil crises in 1973 and 1979, during which the price of oil increased dramatically, Japan was forced to rethink its energy policy. The country adopted strategies to reduce its dependence on oil, including the promotion of energy-saving measures and the development of alternative energy sources such as nuclear energy, natural gas, and renewable energies.

Japan still imports oil from different countries, including the United Arab Emirates and Saudi Arabia, but this oil now accounts for less than 50 percent of the country's primary energy needs, compared with 75 percent in the early 1970s. Coal used to be mined in Japan, but the last mine closed in 2002 because it cost more to mine coal than to buy it from abroad. Coal still contributes 19 percent of Japan's primary energy requirements, but now Japan imports it from Australia, China, and Sakhalin (a Russian island to the north of Hokkaido). Oil and gas reserves in Sakhalin may provide Japan with significant supplies in the future. Natural gas is imported from Indonesia and Brunei, and provides 13 percent of the country's fuel.

DOMESTIC ENERGY SOURCES

Japan has developed nuclear energy in an attempt to reduce energy imports. Although the uranium needed for this must be imported, the amount required is relatively small. Also, the countries from which it is bought, mainly Australia and Canada, are politically stable, which means that the supply of uranium is unlikely to be disrupted by political crises.

◄ The brightly-lit Tokyo skyline shows that Japan is an energy hungry country.

With fifty-one power stations in operation, Japan has the third-largest nuclear energy program in the world, after the United States and France. Approximately 26.9 percent of Japan's electricity is generated by nuclear power, compared with 62 percent generated from fossil fuels. Government plans to expand the country's nuclear energy use by 30 percent by 2010 will require the construction of twelve more reactors. Concerns among the Japanese public about the safety of nuclear power, however, are growing.

▲ A power station located in Tokyo's main harbor uses imported oil as a fuel to generate electricity.

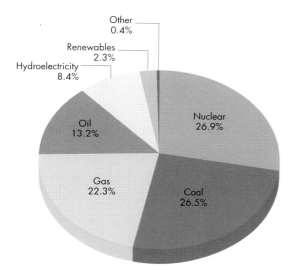

Other 0.4%
Renewables 2.3%
Hydroelectricity 8.4%
Oil 13.2%
Gas 22.3%
Coal 26.5%
Nuclear 26.9%

▲ Electricity production by type

Focus on: The Nuclear Energy Dilemma

Despite the significant role that nuclear power has played in tackling the problem of Japan's dependence on imported oil, the country's nuclear industry faces an uncertain future. The confidence of the Japanese public has been shaken by a series of incidents that have raised concerns about the safety of nuclear power. In 2002, seventeen reactors were shut down when it was discovered that they had not been maintained in line with government regulations. It took two years before they were fully reopened after full checks had been carried out. Then, in 2004, an accident at another reactor claimed the lives of four workers. Those who support nuclear energy argue that this loss of life is no greater than that which results from accidents in other industries. But the 2004 accident, combined with more general fears about the safe disposal of nuclear waste, has increased public opposition to nuclear energy. The Japanese government is attempting to rebuild public confidence in the use of nuclear energy by stressing the role it can play in reducing greenhouse gas emissions. The government will need to win back public support if it hopes to move ahead with its planned expansion of nuclear energy.

Japan's government is carrying out research into alternative sources of energy as part of its policy to tackle the problem of dependence on imported energy and nuclear power. Although the country has many mountain rivers with rapid flow, they are generally too small for large-scale commercial development of hydroelectric power (HEP). At present, HEP is used to generate 8.4 percent of Japan's electricity, and there is little opportunity to expand this. Wind, solar, wave, and geothermal power sources are also being investigated.

RESOURCES FROM LAND AND SEA

Japan lacks mineral resources such as iron ore, copper, and bauxite. These materials are important to industry and, therefore, must be imported. Gold, magnesium, and silver have been found in Japan in sufficient amounts to meet the needs of domestic industries. With over 66 percent of Japan's land area covered by forests, timber is an important domestic resource. But because steep slopes and lack of roads makes access to the forested areas difficult, exploiting them is often costly. It is

Energy Data

- Energy consumption as % of world total: 5.1%
- Energy consumption by sector (% of total):
  Industry: 44
  Transportation: 27
  Agriculture: 3
  Services: 12
  Residential: 14
- CO_2 emissions as % of world total: 5
- CO_2 emissions per capita in tons per year: 10

Source: World Resources Institute

▼ Malaysian timber being handled by a Japanese cargo vessel in Minimata Bay, on Kyushu. Most timber used in Japan is imported.

generally cheaper to import timber. In 2002, over 80 percent of Japan's timber needs were met this way. Japan is the world's largest importer of tropical timber. Environmental groups and local communities in countries such as Cameroon and Papua New Guinea have criticized Japanese companies for the extensive felling of tropical rain forests in these countries.

Historically, fishing has been an essential industry for Japan as an island nation, and has provided both employment and an important source of food for the population. The area of the Pacific Ocean off Japan's east coast, where two currents meet, has provided rich fishing grounds. Since the late 1980s, however, the catch has declined from over 11,810,478 tons (12 million metric tons) in 1989 to just under 5,905,239 tons (6 million metric tons) in 2002. This decline is the result of overfishing and of the drop in numbers of people employed in fishing. In 1953, the fishing workforce was

800,000, but by 2003, it had fallen to 238,000. Younger workers are not replacing older ones when they retire, and over 34 percent of those people who fish commercially in the early twenty-first century are over the age of 65.

Japan's annual consumption of fish remains high, at about 12 million tons (over 11 million metric tons) in 2002, with 165 pounds (75 kilograms) eaten per person, compared with the world average of 35 lbs (16 kg). To meet this demand, Japan's fish imports have risen five-fold over the last twenty years. The increase in imports, which come from China, the United States, Thailand, Indonesia, and Russia, is partly caused by greater demand for luxury types of fish, such as tuna and salmon (rather than mackerel and pollack), which cannot be met from local waters.

▼ Tsukiji Fish Market in Tokyo is one of the largest fish markets in the world. It is a showcase for Japan's long history of using the sea as a resource.

Economy and Income

Japan's economy is made up of two tiers. The first consists of a small number of large and highly efficient manufacturing companies geared to producing goods for export, such as cars and household electrical goods. Many of these companies, such as Toyota and Sony, have become known around the world. Nippon Steel, although not so well-known outside Japan, is the world's second-largest steel producer (after Arcelor of Luxembourg). The second tier consists of small- to medium-sized companies, many of which are family-owned, that produce items for the domestic market or components for the export companies. For example, Morino Industries, based near Tokyo, employs thirty-seven people and makes metal frames for the manufacturers of wide-screen televisions. About 99 percent of Japan's manufacturing firms are smaller companies with 300 or fewer employees.

JAPAN AS A WORLD ECONOMIC POWER

Japan has the world's second largest economy (after the United States). Japan achieved this status during the 1960s and early 1970s, when it had economic growth rates of about 11 percent a year—the highest in the world at the time. This growth was mainly brought about by the tier of large, efficient companies mass-producing consumer goods primarily for the U.S. market. Exports from these companies earned the foreign revenue needed to buy the raw materials that Japan lacked, particularly oil and iron ore. High-technology industries were particularly suited to Japan because they needed only small amounts of raw materials and

energy, and depended on the skilled and well-educated workforce that Japan had developed since the end of World War II. Japan's post-war economic growth was particularly remarkable given the widespread destruction of its industries that had taken place during the war. Some observers to refer to this period as Japan's "economic miracle."

▲ A shipyard in Kobe. Shipbuilding is one of Japan's most important heavy industries. Japan's companies produce ships for both domestic and international markets.

Economic Data

- Gross National Income (GNI) in U.S.$: 4.7 trillion
- World rank by GNI: 2
- GNI per capita in U.S.$: 37,810
- World rank by GNI per capita: 9
- Economic growth: 2.7%

Source: World Bank

As with other wealthy nations, Japan's economic development has been in the manufacturing and service sectors, both of which tend to be based in cities. The rural sectors of agriculture and forestry have shrunk, and employment in the industries that produce and provide raw materials dropped from 37 percent of the labor force in 1975 to 4.6 percent in 2003. Japan's agricultural land is very productive, with crop yields per acre among the highest in the world. However, only about 15 percent of the country's land area is suitable for farming, and much of it is too expensive to be used for agriculture. The amount of food that Japan grows for itself has declined significantly, because it is cheaper to import food from the United States and China. In 2003, Japan produced only about 40 percent of its own food, compared to 75 percent in 1965.

RECESSION AND ITS AFTERMATH

During the 1990s, the country's impressive economic growth rates slowed dramatically. The economy grew at only 1 percent or less per year. This recession was partly caused by changes in the exchange rate system that existed between Japan and the United States. In 1985, the Plaza Accord devalued the U.S. dollar, changing its value in relation to the yen. After the Accord, the U.S. dollar was worth 120 yen, about one-third of its value in 1970. Japanese export goods became more expensive and less competitive in the global

 Did You Know?

In spite of the "lost decade," Japan is still a major economic power in the world. In 2003, Japan's exports accounted for 5.9 percent of the world trade in goods and services and for 5.23 percent of global imports.

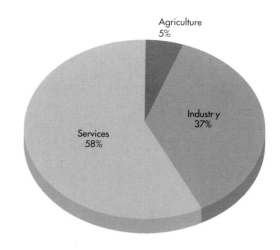

Agriculture 5%
Industry 37%
Services 58%

▲ Contribution by sector to national income

▲ The Roppongi Hills complex, in Tokyo, is a model for Japan's future, turning part of the city into a modern business, retail, and entertainment center.

market. This change led Japanese companies to shift much of their production to places with cheap labor rates, such as Southeast Asia and China. For some time, Japanese companies were able to continue to sell their goods cheaply, but problems began to arise as the countries in which the goods were manufactured began to produce cheaper versions of high-tech goods.

By the early 1990s, Japan could not compete with these rivals. It was also heavily dependent on the global rather than the domestic market, partly because its manufacturing capacity had been much reduced. Since the end of the 1990s, the country's economic situation has shown signs of recovery as Japan's companies have started

▼ One way that Japan's companies have maintained their competitiveness is by setting up overseas factories in which labor costs are lower. This Sony television production line is in Vietnam.

to develop strategies such as "one-of-a-kind" production to deal with the challenges posed by the increased competition they face.

Throughout Japan's history, its unemployment rate has usually been low. During the years of the economic miracle, the rate was between 2.1 and 2.8 percent. During the 1990s, however, it rose to 5.6 percent, although this rate was still below that of many European Union countries. Japan's national unemployment figure is now 4.4 percent, but there are variations between social groups. Rates are higher for young people; 9.3 percent of people between the ages of 15 and 24 were out of work in 2004.

WOMEN IN THE WORKFORCE

Traditional attitudes about the role of women in Japanese society mean that, although women now make up about 40 percent of the workforce, they still only fill about 9 percent

of management jobs, and they only get paid 59 percent of men's wages. Measures to tackle such discrimination include the Equal Employment Opportunities Law for Men and Women, passed in 1986. But when jobs in Japan are few—for example, during a recession—the country's women tend to lose out. Because of the cultural resistance to women having careers, the law tends to be ignored. However, there is growing awareness in Japanese society that more working women will be needed in the future when the number of economically active people is likely to drop because of the country's ageing population.

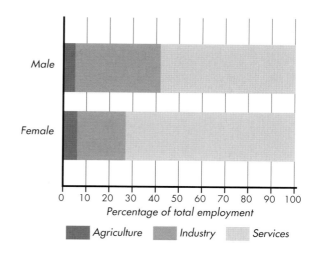

▲ Labor force by sector and gender

Focus on: "One-of-a-kind" Products

The "lost decade" prompted many of Japan's leading companies to develop strategies to tackle the competition they face. Japan's large electronics companies, such as Sharp, are developing "one-of-a-kind" products to compete with the low-cost mass produced goods in the factories of South Korea, Taiwan, and China. They are searching for new technological niches for products that demand high-tech precision and advanced manufacturing techniques. For example, in 2005, Sharp announced the development of a split LCD screen for televisions that would allow two people to watch different programs or use different functions (such as TV viewing or computer monitoring) at the same time. Companies that produce "one-of-a-kind" goods must keep their manufacturing techniques secret. This often means using them only in domestic factories, rather than overseas, where it may harder to protect them from their rivals. Many companies are investing in research to develop high-quality niche products. For example, in 2005, Canon established a research center near Tokyo and a new factory for making top-of-the-line digital cameras in Oita prefecture.

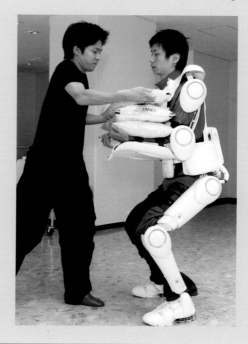

► This robot suit was developed by Professor Yoshiyuki Sankai to assist the elderly in their everyday lives by giving them twice their usual strength.

CHAPTER 8

Global Connections

Many of Japan's leading companies, such as Toshiba and Canon, invest in other countries by setting up factories there. Or they may invest their money in an overseas company in return for a share in the profits and a degree of control over what the company does. Some companies, such as Honda, have cut transportation costs of their goods by moving closer to customer demand. For example, Honda has a large factory in Swindon, in Britain, which is an excellent location because it is close to numerous customers in the heavily populated south of England. By moving production to countries such as China, Taiwan, and South Korea, Japanese companies have benefited from wage rates between twenty and thirty times lower than those in Japan. In the last decade, however, Japanese companies have found themselves in competition with the companies of these countries, which can produce the same goods as Japanese companies for an even lower price. The result is that some Japanese companies have cut back on their overseas low-cost production and are concentrating on high-tech precision manufacturing within their own country.

OVERSEAS DEVELOPMENT AID

Since the 1980s, Japan has been one of the most generous countries in the world in giving overseas development aid (ODA). ODA is given in various ways, including grants of money, technical help, and loans. It is an important part of Japan's foreign policy, partly because the aid is often given with certain "strings" attached. Countries receiving the ODA from Japan must usually, in return, allow Japan access to its natural resources. For example, Indonesia, which has received a lot of aid from Japan during the past ten years, in return provides Japan with much of the tropical hardwood it needs. However, in spite of the political importance of ODA, Japan has been cutting the amount it gives since 1999. That year, it stood at about $11 billion, but by 2003, the amount had fallen to $8.9 billion. This is a result of the domestic economic problems Japan has faced. Nevertheless, Japan remains the second biggest ODA donor in the world, after the United States. Japan has also hosted international aid conferences, such as the United Nations World Conference on Disaster Reduction, held in Kobe in 2005, which focused on how to help poorer countries deal with threats posed by natural disasters.

▲ Containerization has benefited trade in Japan by allowing for the rapid handling and shipping of goods. Within minutes of docking this ship will start unloading.

JAPAN IN THE GLOBAL COMMUNITY

As its economy relies heavily on imported energy and access to world markets, Japan needs to remain on good terms with as many countries as possible. To keep relations with other countries strong, Japan is an active member of a number of global groups and organizations, including the G8 (a group made up of the eight largest industrialized countries in the world), the World Bank, and the Organization for Economic Cooperation and Development (OECD). Japan also takes part in every important international gathering, often in a prominent role. For example, an international conference to tackle climate change was held in Kyoto in 1997. The result was the Kyoto Protocol, which has become the focus for much international debate about the need to reduce greenhouse gas emissions.

 Did You Know?

Japan has been a member of the United Nations since 1956. In 2005, the United States supported Japan's application to become a permanent member of the UN Security Council. This would give Japan more influence in discussions of international conflicts and disputes where military intervention or economic sanctions may have to be used.

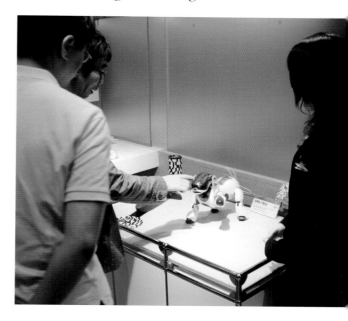

▲ Visitors to a Sony showroom admire Aibo, the robotic dog, one of the latest Japanese electronic products. Electronic products make up a great deal of the country's exports.

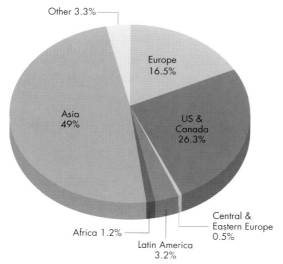

▲ Destination of exports by major trading region

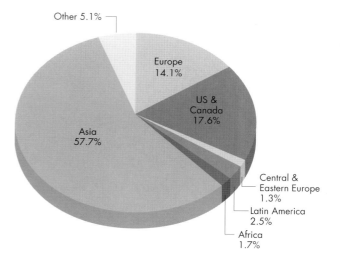

▲ Origin of imports by major trading region

▲ Universal Studios, in Osaka. This American-style theme park is one example of the close ties between Japan and the United States.

Since 2001, Japan's government has further extended the country's involvement in the global community. Japan's long-term alliance with the United States is partly the reason for this. Since the end of World War II, the United States has provided a military shield for the defense of Japan and, beginning in 2004, has worked with Japan on developing a missile defense system. The two countries often work together on foreign policy issues, for example, on how to deal with security threats from North Korea. Japan's concerns about its neighbor were heightened in 1998, when North Korea fired a medium-range missile over Japan and into the Pacific. Since then, Japan and the United States, along with China, Russia, and South Korea, have met with North Korea several times to try to convince North Korea to give up its nuclear program in return for economic aid and guarantees of security. As of early 2006, there has been no progress, and it is this situation that has led some to argue that Japan needs to arm itself.

Japan's relations with its neighbors are politically and economically significant, but they are also stormy. There are ongoing territorial disputes, and resentment of Japan's conduct during World War II frequently flare up. For example, in 2005, China and South Korea reacted angrily to approval by Japan's Ministry of Education of history textbooks that omitted reference to wartime atrocities committed by Japanese soldiers. But there are also positive connections, including the fact that many of the tourists who visit Japan come from within the East Asian region.

POPULAR CULTURE, SPORTS, AND TECHNOLOGY

During about the past fifty years, the West has strongly influenced Japanese culture. Fast food items, such as hamburgers, have become widely available; American leisure activities, most notably baseball, have become popular. South Korean food, music, actors, and television soap operas are also popular in Japan.

There has also been a growing interest in Japanese culture from outside Japan. Judo and kendo have gained Olympic status. Karaoke singing is popular, and collecting *Pokemon* cards was a worldwide trend. Some types of Japanese food have become very popular in the United States and Britain. Particularly widespread are sushi bars, which offer a range of foods based on rice and raw fish. Also, Japanese companies have played a leading role in the production of video-game consoles (for example, Nintendo), photocopiers, and digital cameras, and DVDs.

Japan has played an increasingly prominent role in international sports, hosting the Winter Olympics in 1998 and cohosting (with South Korea) the 2002 soccer World Cup. The next major event that Japan will host is the Rugby World Cup in 2011. Some Japanese baseball players have become famous outside Japan by playing for major league teams in the United States. Hideki Matsui, for example, plays for the New York Yankees, and Ichiro Suzuki plays for the Seattle Mariners.

▲ Ryoko Tamura of Japan (wearing white) defeated Feng Gao of China to become world judo champion at the 2003 championship held in Osaka.

Focus on: Japan's Changing Relationship with China

Until recently, Japan was the most powerful nation in East Asia. But the balance of power is shifting as China's economy grows. In the early twenty-first century, China has begun to compete with Japan for regional influence and resources, particularly energy. Although they are major trading partners, a number of political issues have given rise to tensions between Japan and China. For example, many in Japan see China's increase in military spending as a threat, while China fears that Japan is abandoning its pacifist stance and drawing closer to the United States to help contain China's growing regional influence. Many Chinese feel that Japan has still not shown remorse about World War II atrocities, and anti-Japanese feeling is common in China. Some experts, however, believe it suits China's government to use Japan as a scapegoat because it distracts attention from China's own domestic problems, such as China's growing inequality in income.

CHAPTER 9

Transportation and Communications

Despite the difficulties posed by its mountainous terrain, Japan has good transport links, and the country's engineers are expert at building bridges and tunnels. Japan's transportation networks must be constructed in a way that minimizes the impact of earthquakes. Overall, Japan has spent a great deal of money on increasing accessibility across the country. In some areas, however—particularly rural areas—many of its roads go nowhere. This is because they were built as part of schemes set up by LDP politicians in order to win votes. These roads were not needed, but they provided jobs in the construction industry.

RAIL AND ROAD

Japan is famous for its high-speed trains, which are known as *shinkansen*, or bullet trains. The national rail network includes ordinary trains as well as shinkansen. It is extensive, and carries more than 21 billion passengers a year. In 1988, Japan's four main islands were joined by rail with the completion of a tunnel linking Honshu with Hokkaido and a bridge linking Honshu with Shikoku. Rail lines that link cities with their suburbs are particularly popular, with more than 70 percent of office workers in the main cities using them. In nine cities, these commuter lines connect with subway lines, enabling people to continue their journey by rail within the cities.

Japan's road network consists of expressways, or major roads linking towns and cities, and ordinary roads. Expressways link the main cities and, like railroads, cross difficult terrain and are built to withstand earthquakes. Construction costs for Japan's expressways, not surprisingly, are among the highest in the world, and tolls are charged for using them. Over 95 percent of Japan's freight is transported by road. In the 1960s, car ownership began to increase in Japan, brought about by increasing incomes and improvements in roads. Japanese companies began producing small, fuel-efficient cars because fuel is expensive in the country as a result of oil having to be imported. Car

▼ The Akashi Kaikyo suspension bridge provides a vital transportation link between the islands of Honshu and Awaji-shima. Measuring 12,828 ft (3,910 m), it is the longest suspension bridge in the world.

ownership in Japan continues to rise. In 1990, around 35 million Japanese people owned cars; by 2002, this figure had increased to over 54 million.

Tokyo suffers from serious problems of traffic congestion and air pollution caused by vehicle emissions. Strict regulations have been created, particularly on vehicle exhaust emissions. Vehicles are tested regularly to ensure that their emissions of nitrogen oxide (NO_x) do not exceed a certain level. Although individual vehicles now emit much less NO_x than used to be the case, the increase in the number of cars on the road has raised levels of NO_x in the atmosphere in spite of the regulations.

Transport & Communications Data

- Total roads: 731,560 miles/1,177,278 km
- Total paved roads: 568,422 miles/ 914,745 km
- Total unpaved roads: 163,138 miles/ 262,533 km
- Total railways: 14,651 miles/23,577 km
- Major airports: 174
- Cars per 1000 people: 428
- Cellular phones per 1000 people: 679
- Personal computers per 1000 people: 382
- Internet users per 1000 people: 483

Source: World Bank and CIA World Factbook

Focus on: Bullet Trains (*Shinkansen*)

Japan was the first country to develop a high-speed rail system with special track. The first section of high-speed track was opened in 1964, with the first bullet trains running at speeds of up to 125 miles per hour (200 kilometers per hour). New models of train have been built since then, and these new models regularly run at speeds up to 185 mph (300 kph). Called *shinkansen* in Japan (meaning "New Trunk Line"), these trains can be up to sixteen cars long. *Shinkansen* service is efficient and reliable. In 2003, its average arrival time was within six seconds of the scheduled time. The track and overhead wires (which carry the electricity that powers the trains) are monitored by high-speed test trains fitted with special equipment that run during the night so that they do no disrupt daytime services.

◀ Japan's bullet trains have been copied around the world because of their high speed and efficiency. They provide passengers with a high level of comfort and nearly always run full.

AIR AND SEA

Between the 1980s and 2000, air transportation in Japan grew significantly, and the number of travelers from other countries entering Japan tripled. Various factors, including recession and the threat of terrorism, led to a 9 percent drop in travel to Japan between 2000 and 2001. Fears of SARS, a new contagious disease, and the continuing threat of terrorism prompted a further decrease in 2003.

The top foreign destinations for Japanese travelers are the United States, China, and South Korea. At the same time, the number of people flying within Japan has more than doubled during the past twenty years. The most heavily traveled domestic route is between Tokyo and Sapporo. In the past ten years, airports have expanded to meet demand. The largest is New Tokyo International, about 37 miles (60 km) outside Tokyo, which handles more than 30 million passengers and 2.2 million tons (2 million metric tons) of freight a year.

Because Japan is surrounded by sea, water transportation is important, and the country has huge ports. Until the oil crises in the 1970s, almost all imports and exports were transported by sea. With increases in costs and changes in industrial demand toward lightweight technological components, some international freight is now transported by air.

Did You Know?

Chubu Centrair International Airport, located near Tokonamo City, opened in February 2005. It is the newest of three international airports in Japan and is built on an artificial island. The island is constructed in the shape of a "D,"so that sea currents inside Ise Bay flow freely around it. The island's shores are partially constructed with natural rocks and are sloped to allow coastal habitats to develop on them, as they do on the naturally occurring rocky shores found in this area.

▼ Kansei International Airport serves the cities of Osaka, Kyoto, and Kobe, located in southern Japan. It is one of Japan's main airports, and it is built entirely on land reclaimed from the sea.

COMMUNICATIONS AND INFORMATION

The rate at which communications technology is being adopted in Japan has accelerated over the past ten years. Mobile phone ownership rose from four million in 1995 to over 86 million in 2003. The Internet, which came into commercial use in Japan in 1993, is widely used by more than 77 million individuals in Japan, and 88 percent of all households have Internet access. Within the population, people between 13 and 19 years old have the highest rate of Internet use: over 91 percent. The government wants to promote the use of high-speed Internet in schools. It also wants to improve information literacy among the general population by installing terminals in public facilities. The number of high-speed Internet users in Japan has grown particularly fast since 2001. Japan now has the third-highest number of high-speed subscribers in the world, following the United States and South Korea.

Japan has one of the highest newspaper circulations in the world, with 50 million newspapers sold each day. The country has five general daily papers, including *Yomiuri Shimbun* and *Asahi Shimbun*, and three English-language dailies, including the *Japan Times*. Most newspapers are delivered to homes or offices rather than bought at newstands. Television ownership is very high, and many

channels are available. TV broadcasts in Japan can be received with an aerial, through a cable, or with a satellite dish. Recent developments include the promotion of digital broadcasting. The government aims to switch from analog to digital by 2011.

▲ Cell phones that offer Internet and other information services are everywhere in Japan.

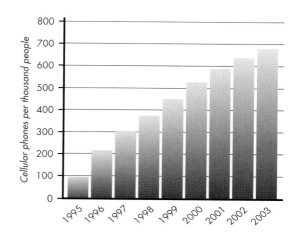

▲ Cellular phone use, 1995–2003

Did You Know?

Japan's most popular Web site is Channel 2. With comments to the site posted by more than one million people every day, Channel 2 provides people with the opportunity to highlight news that does not get mentioned in the mainstream media. It also give people the chance to express their feelings about their lives. They may remain anonymous, if they wish.

CHAPTER 10

Education and Health

The 1947 School Education Act defined the structure of the education system in Japan. It established that schooling is compulsory for children from the age of 6 to 15. Children spend the first six years in elementary school and then advance to junior high school. After junior high school, students must pass a competitive entrance exam if they wish to attend senior high school. In 2003, 97 percent of junior-high graduates passed this exam. After three years of senior high school, students may go on to higher education. They can choose from a range of different institutions, including colleges of technology, which offer vocational courses, and universities, which offer academic courses. In 2003, about 46 percent of senior high school graduates moved on to these institutions. Students not going to college or university may get jobs. During the recession years of the 1990s, however, the number of jobs available to them fell, and they suffered higher unemployment than college and university graduates. University graduates have better career opportunities. For example, they may become scientists, doctors, lawyers, or accountants.

CONTROVERSY AND CHANGE IN EDUCATION

Japan has a national curriculum that outlines what is to be taught in schools. It is revised every ten years. The Ministry of Education, Culture, Sports, Science, and Technology, which standardizes education across the country, regulates the textbooks used in Japan's schools. This ministry, therefore, has great power over what material is considered suitable for students. In 2005, the ministry's approval of a certain history textbook led to a heated international argument. This particular book did not mention the brutal acts carried out by Japanese soldiers against the citizens of China and South Korea during the 1930s and 1940s. Even though many of Japan's schools shunned the book, people in China and South Korea were outraged that it had been approved.

In Japan, traditional educational values and practices emphasize conformity, rote learning, and group discipline rather than individual performance. There is little room for students

◀ A typical elementary school class in Japan. Schools in Japan are well-equipped, and the country has high standards of education.

to pursue their own interests because the curriculum is predetermined and testing of achievement is very rigid. However, there are signs that this may be changing. Some high schools are allowing students to choose some of the courses that they take. In early 2006, this opportunity was only available to students in schools serving poor areas with relatively high truancy rates and low academic results. If it proves successful, however, it may be adopted in other parts of Japan's educational system.

There is a growing demand in Japan for equality between the sexes in education. In 1998, 26 percent of young women in Japan attended universities (compared to 15 percent in 1990), but this was still fewer than the 35 percent of young men who enrolled that year. During the recent recession, female graduates found it harder than males to get jobs. Also, the career path for most women is shorter than for men, because women often have to leave paid employment when they have children. When their children are older, women may wish to return to paid employment but are often forced

to take lower paying and less satisfying jobs. Older women may then have to leave their jobs again to care for their elderly parents and, often, the parents of their husbands.

? Did You Know?

In 2002, Japan's school week was reduced from six days to five in order to to give young people more free time to pursue their own interests.

Education and Health Data

- Life expectancy at birth, male: 78.2
- Life expectancy at birth, female: 85.3
- Infant mortality rate per 1,000: 3
- Under-five mortality rate per 1,000: 4
- Physicians per 1,000 people: 2
- Health expenditure as % of GDP: 7.9%
- Education expenditure as % of GDP: 3.6%
- Primary net enrollment: 100%
- Student-teacher ratio, primary school: 20
- Adult literacy as % age 15+: 99%

Source: United Nations Agencies and World Bank

◀ These high school students are taking part in an annual sports day. In most of Japan's schools, such days are a highlight of the school year. Teams of children compete in sports events and perform artistic displays.

Although education is highly valued by Japan's government and its society in general, it does not determine success within society, which is still strongly influenced by gender and the social class of parents. The changing of cultural norms; such as the shift away from the notion of the importance of the group towards that of the individual; advances in science and technology; and economic globalization are all challenges the Japanese educational system will have to address in the future.

TRENDS IN HEALTH

Japan's women now have the highest life expectancy at birth of any group in the world. In 1970, their life expectancy was 74 years; by 2003, it had risen to 85. Over the same period, life expectancy for Japan's men also rose, from 69 to 78. Japan now has the third highest overall life expectancy in the world, after Iceland and Hong Kong. These increases are mainly a result of the development of a comprehensive and well-equipped medical system and advances in medical technology. The major causes of death in Japan have changed from tuberculosis, in 1950, to cancer and heart disease, in 2005. Evidence suggests that increases in cancer and heart disease are linked to lifestyle habits such as smoking (30 percent of Japan's adults smoke, compared with 17 percent in the United States) and eating fast foods that are high in fats, such as burgers and fries. The traditional diet of Japan, which is based around fish and is low in fats and sugars, is

▼ A sushi bar in Tokyo serves one type of traditional Japanese food.

healthy and probably accounts for the low obesity rate in Japan. In 2003, only 3.6 percent of Japan's adult population was classified as obese, compared with 23 percent in Britain and 31 percent in the United States.

Japan's health-care system is financed by health insurance and run by the government. It was established in 1961, and all adults participate, mainly through employers' programs or local-authority programs for the retired. It has generally been very successful, but it will be put under strain in the future as a result of the country's aging population; 25 percent of the population will be over age 65 by 2020. One government proposal is to set up specific health-insurance programs for people over a certain age. Some older people need, for example, their food cooked and their clothes washed for them more than they need medicines or operations.

With the traditional role of women in families changing, the pressures on the government to tackle care of the elderly look set to increase.

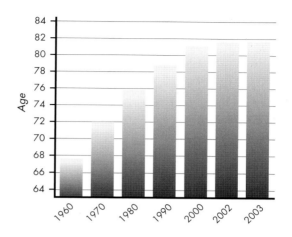

▲ Life expectancy at birth, 1960–2003

▶ An 81-year-old man in Japan checks his blood pressure in a hospital using a self-test machine.

Focus on: Minamata Disease

During the 1960s, a number of cases of industrial pollution caused deaths or serious health problems. Perhaps the best known of these cases is that of Minamata Bay, where between 1932 and 1968, a local company dumped mercury into the ocean. During this period, about 100,000 local people for whom fish from the bay was a staple food became ill with symptoms of mercury poisoning, including slurred speech and spasms of the legs and arms, and many died. It was not until 1968 that the source of "Minamata Disease" was recognized. The company that dumped the mercury was taken to court in 1969. Since this case, Japan has become more aware of the dangers of uncontrolled industrial pollution and laws, such as the 1970 Waste Management and Public Cleansing Law, have been passed to prevent the dumping of toxic wastes.

CHAPTER 11

Culture and Religion

Japanese culture is a rich blend of traditional Asian and modern Western influences. The Western influences generally date from World War II, when lifestyles changed significantly and many people moved to cities to work in factories and offices. This change in economic conditions has affected Japanese culture in many ways.

ARCHITECTURE

Historically, Japanese architecture was influenced by Chinese styles. The main building material was wood. The oldest wooden structures in the world date from A.D. 670 and can be found at the Buddhist temple in Horyuji. Traditional wooden Japanese houses are often constructed on pillars to allow air to circulate underneath them. This keeps the houses cool, particularly in the south

of the country, with its hot, humid summers. The interior space of these houses is open; opaque paper-covered sliding panels are used to divide the space when necessary. Straw mats called *tatami* provide a floor covering that is cool in the summer, warm in winter, and fresher than carpet in the humid months. Today, modern houses, especially in cities, are likely to be built of concrete and have interior walls, but many still have a *tatami* mat room, which is used for relaxation. Buildings in cities tend to be modern, high-tech, and multistoried, so that maximum use is made of the limited urban space. Many of them were built after the

▼ People pray during a service at Higashi Honganjii, a Buddhist temple in Kyoto. The floor is covered with traditional *tatami* mats made of straw. Shoes must be removed to walk on a *tatami* floor.

end of World War II. Driven by the need to rebuild, architects and planners used readily available new building materials—including steel, glass, and concrete—rather than traditional materials.

CLOTHING AND CUISINE

Traditional Japanese dress for men, women, and children is the kimono. Kimonos usually are made from silk; have long sleeves; fall to the ankle; and are tied around the waist with a wide belt called an obi. Women's kimonos are more elaborate than men's, consisting of twelve

▲ The traditional Japanese kimono is still worn by some women, but the majority of Japanese people wear Western-style clothing.

separate pieces that have to be put on in a particular order. A lightweight and less formal kimono, called *yukata*, may be worn by children. Today, kimonos are worn mainly on ceremonial occasions, such as weddings, while Western-style clothes—such as T-shirts, jeans, skirts, and dresses—are more commonly worn for everyday purposes.

Japanese cuisine is dominated by white rice. All other foods served with it, such as fish, meat, or vegetables, are regarded as side dishes. Different traditional cooking techniques, such as grilling or simmering, are used to prepare these side dishes, but some, like sashimi (fish), are just left raw. Seafood dishes, including sashimi (thinly sliced raw fish) and sushi are very popular. Other specialities include miso soup, tempura, and pickled vegetables. Japan's traditional diet has been affected by Western influences, and foods such as pasta, noodles, and bread are common. Fast food is also popular.

❓ Did You Know?

Traditional Japanese meals are named after the number of side dishes. For example, *ichiju-sansai* means "one soup, three side dishes."

MUSIC AND THE PERFORMING ARTS

Japan's tradition of classical music dates from the seventh century. This style of music is played on instruments such as the lute-like *shamisen* and the *koto*, which is like a zither. More recently, Western classical music has become popular in Japan, and the country now has some world-class classical musicians, such as conductor Ozawa Seiji. Traditional Japanese music has lost popularity, and the number of players of traditional instruments has dropped.

Both Japanese and Western popular music styles have huge followings in Japan. Western pop music was introduced in Japan after World War II. From it developed a style of Japanese pop music that uses the pentatonic scale to produce catchy Western-style melodies.

RELIGIOUS BELIEFS

Japan has two main religions: Shintoism and Buddhism. These religions have coexisted with each other since the introduction of Buddhism to the country in the sixth century. Shinto beliefs and traditions existed before this time, but unlike other major religions, Shintoism had no written scriptures. Buddhism provided a framework of doctrine but still permitted the belief in many gods that is central to Shintoism. A particular form of Buddhism, called Zen, has developed in Japan. Zen Buddhism emphasizes self-discipline and meditation. Today, 94.6 percent of Japanese people say they believe in both of these religions, although religious practice is not widespread. Many people in Japan, however, use religious ceremonies to celebrate births, marriages, and deaths, as well as to mark the New Year.

In 1549, Francis Xavier, a Jesuit missionary, brought Christianity to Japan. At first, Japan's ruler, Toyotomi Hideyoshi, tolerated it. By 1614, the number of Christians in Japan had grown to more than 300,000, and the shogun, Tokugawa Ieyasu, became concerned about its popularity. Christians in Japan were persecuted for about 200 years, until the religion was accepted again in 1859. Since then, the number of Christians has grown to more than 3 million. Christianity is not compatible Japan's traditional religions because it does not allow worship of more than one god.

▲ Senso-ji, in Tokyo, is one of the most visited Buddhist temples in Japan and dates back to the mid-seventh century. Like many Buddhist temple complexes in Japan, it also has a Shinto shrine.

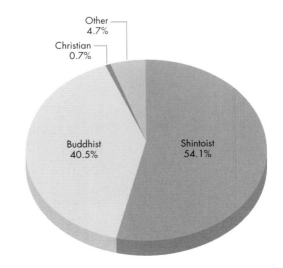

Other 4.7%
Christian 0.7%
Buddhist 40.5%
Shintoist 54.1%

▲ Japan's major religions

► Actors in Kabuki theater create and apply their own make-up using traditional methods. The colorful drama of Kabuki is popular in Japan, and Kabuki has become one of Japan's major tourist attractions.

A noticeable trend in Japan since the late 1980s has been the rise in the number of religious cults. A cult is usually founded by an individual who promotes himself as a living deity and whose followers revere his teachings. In 1995, concerns grew that some cults pose a threat to Japanese society when members of a cult called Aum Shinrikyo released poison gas in the subways of Tokyo, killing twelve people and injuring more than 5,000. The leader of this cult, Shoko Asaharato, was sentenced to death for murder in 2004.

 Did You Know?

Noh is the oldest form of musical theater in Japan. It tells a story through dialogue, song, and dance. The actors in Noh theater dress in colorful costumes and use decorated masks to switch between characters.

Focus on: The Tea Ceremony

The Japanese tea ceremony involves the preparation and serving of green tea in the presence of guests. It is a traditional ritual embodying the principles of Zen Buddhism. The main objective of the ceremony is to become completely focused on the actions of the tea-maker and the utensils being used, so that all present are living in the moment rather than having thoughts of other things and places. Participants in the Japanese tea ceremony believe that this state of mind is spiritually uplifting and allows them to appreciate what is sacred in everyday actions and objects. Few formal tea ceremonies are performed in Japan today, but many Japanese people attend tea schools to learn how to perform the traditional ceremony.

CHAPTER 12

Leisure and Tourism

Leisure time in Japan has increased over about the past ten years. A two-day weekend has been established instead of just one day, and the country's number of public holidays has increased. Japanese employees, however, take only about half their holiday allowances because of a cultural expectation to work long hours. Also, in 1997, an amendment to the Labor Standards Law reduced in the number of overtime hours Japanese work.

Some families in Japan spend a lot of time together, although many fathers do not see their children much because of the pressures of work. Much family leisure time is spent at home, where many people watch TV and play computer games, or on outings, during which people may visit a theme park, play baseball, or go swimming.

Annual events, most of which have a traditional importance, provide opportunities throughout the year for Japanese families to celebrate with one another. For example, when the country's cherry trees flower in April, many families picnic under them and admire the blossoms. At the traditional Buddhist *O-bon* festival, in August, the souls of ancestors are welcomed into homes where fires are lit to greet them. Many businesses close down at this time, and people travel to visit their families to celebrate *O-bon* together.

▼ The Tokyo Dome is one of the largest baseball stadiums in Japan and attracts sell-out crowds for top-level professional games.

LEISURE ACTIVITIES

Sporting activities in Japan—including jogging, soccer, and table tennis—tend to be dominated by men. Sports are very popular in the country, with more than two million joggers and more than one million table-tennis players. Winter sports are also popular in the country, particularly skiing and snowboarding. A number of resorts for these activities exist in the Japanese Alps and on Hokkaido.

Japan's sporting facilities are generally good. The world's largest artificial ski slope is located near Tokyo. All of the country's major cities have at least one stadium for spectator sports, such as baseball, which is one of the most popular sports to watch and play. Baseball was introduced to Japan in 1872 and has been played in the country's schools ever since.

Japan has twelve professional baseball teams, including the Yomiuri Giants and the Seibu Lions, which play in two national leagues. Soccer has become popular in recent years. Japan and South Korea co-hosted the 2002 World Cup, and interest in Japan was high during this time.

Tourism in Japan

- Tourist arrivals, millions: 5.212
- Earnings from tourism in U.S.$: 11,475,000,320
- Tourism as % foreign earnings: 2.2
- Tourist departures, millions: 13.296
- Expenditure on tourism in U.S.$: 36,506,001,408

Source: World Bank

Did You Know?

Comic strips, known as *manga*, are very popular in Japan. *Manga* are published in weekly magazines and generally tell stories. Different types of *manga* are aimed at different audiences. Some are used to help preschool children learn to read, while others specialize in jokes and humor for adults.

▼ Japanese comics (*manga*) for sale on a newsstand. *Manga* are sold throughout the country in locations ranging from convenience stores to *manga* specialty stores.

▲ Bathers enjoy a hot-spring bath (*onsen*) in Kirishima-Yaku national park, on Kyushu. The water is heated by the geothermal activity of the nearby Kirishima volcano.

Other leisure interests include *pachinko*, a form of pinball. *Pachinko* arcades are widespread throughout the towns and cities of Japan and the industry is worth over U.S.$1 billion dollars. It is a form of gambling and, although it is a harmless leisure pursuit for most players, some become addicted and get into serious debt.

Movies in Japan tend to be less successful than television, but recently a number of animated films made in Japan have become popular at home and abroad. Successful Japanese movies include *The Princess Mononoke*, made in 1997, which attracted more than 12 million viewers in Japan, and *Spirited Away*, which won an Oscar for the best animated film in 2003. On television, animated shows (*animes*) are also popular. *Animes* such as *Astro Boy* and

Dragonball Z have also been exported to other countries, including the United States.

VACATIONS AT HOME AND ABROAD

Day trips and holidays in Japan are popular. The country's varied landscape provides many attractions, and activities that have been developed to take advantage of it. For example, there are about 3,000 spa resorts, such as Ikaho, which is located 80 miles (129 km) north of Tokyo. People visit the spas to bathe in the hot mineral waters. The country also has many theme parks, which attract both domestic and foreign visitors. These parks include Yoshimoto Shotenjai (Laughter Street), in Osaka, and Tokyo Disneyland.

Until recently, increasing numbers of Japanese had been traveling abroad. Their most popular destinations were the United States, China, and South Korea. But over the past six years this trend has slowed as a result of economic recession and world events, such as the September 11, 2001, terrorist attacks in the United States. Foreign visitors to Japan have been relatively few because, until recently, traveling to Japan was too expensive for most tourists. In 2003, Japan had just over 5 million tourists, while France had 77 million. Overseas tourists visit Japan to enjoy the variety of scenery (such as mountains and lakes) and to take part in or observe cultural events such as cherry-blossom viewing. Most foreign tourists in Japan come from nearby Asian countries. For example, in 2003, 28 percent came from South Korea and 15 percent came from Taiwan. Twelve percent of Japan's foreign tourists came from the United States, 3.8 percent came from Britain, and 1.8 percent came from Germany.

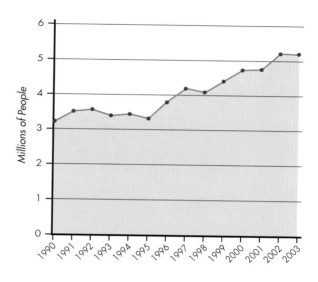

▲ Changes in international tourism, 1990–2002

Focus on: Sumo Wrestling

Historical sources show that sumo wrestling has existed in Japan for nearly 2,000 years. In this sport, two men wearing only colorful *mawashi* (belly bands) wrestle with each other on a floor of sand and clay. Each wrestler aims to make his opponent leave the ring or touch the ground with any part of his body other than the soles of his feet.

Sumo wrestlers, who wear their hair styled like ancient warriors, weigh between 220 and 617 pounds (100–280 kg). All practicing sumo wrestlers must belong to a training stable in which they are traditionally subject to many rules and regulations about what to eat and how to behave. Although sumo wrestling is still one of Japan's most popular spectator sports, fewer young boys seem to want to take it up today. This may be because the wearing of the *mawashi* is seen as "uncool." It has been suggested that boys should be allowed to wear sumo pants, which are like cycling shorts, but many traditionalists strongly oppose this.

◀ Two sumo wrestlers prepare for a bout at the National Sumo Stadium in Ryogoku, Tokyo.

CHAPTER 13

Environment and Conservation

During the 1960s and 1970s, Japan had very serious pollution problems resulting from rapid industrialization and the belief that economic growth was more important than protection of the environment. Japan's government and the country's businesses seemed unaware of the dangers. In some cases, even when the damage was obvious, economic growth and profit took priority. In the 1960s, a factory discharged mercury into the Agano River, in Niigata, poisoning fish and the local people who ate them. During the same decade, a petrochemical plant in Yokkaiichi released sulphur dioxide, causing high levels of smog and widespread respiratory disease in people living near the plant.

▲ Emissions from industrial complexes such as this one in Kawasaki add to the problem of air pollution in Japan.

AIR POLLUTION

Since the 1960s, Japan's air and water quality have been considerably improved. Measures have been introduced to monitor and control industrial emissions and to manage industrial waste disposal. For example, in 1968, the Air Pollution Control Act was passed and air quality monitoring stations were established. These laws ensure that levels of pollutants, such as sulphur dioxide, are not exceeded. In spite of such measures, however, Japan was still the world's fourth largest producer of greenhouse gases (after the United States, China, and Russia) in 2004. Urban air pollution is a particular problem, even though Japan has strict vehicle-emissions standards that ensure that vehicles have catalytic converters and use high quality fuel.

WATER POLLUTION

Although many of Japan's rivers are now cleaner, water quality in lakes and enclosed coastal waters is generally poor, with 25 percent of lakes and reservoirs affected by algae blooms. These regularly occur when rainfall washes fertilizers off agricultural land. Clean water supplies are limited. The difficulties of building reservoirs where rivers are short and gradients are steep mean that only 20 percent of the country's potential fresh water resources are stored and used. During the period of rapid industrialization in the 1960s, much of the ground water used for urban supplies was polluted by chemicals used in the manufacture of circuit boards for computers. Over about the past decade, much manufacturing of this type

Environmental and Conservation Data

📁 Forested area as % total land area: 56.7
📁 Protected area as % total land area: 14
📁 Number of protected areas: 770

SPECIES DIVERSITY

Category	Known species	Threatened species
Mammals	188	37
Breeding birds	210	34
Reptiles	92	11
Amphibians	64	10
Fish	1,007	13
Plants	5,565	11

Source: World Resources Institute

has been relocated to China and Southeast Asia. This change has led to further decreases in the levels of industrial pollution in Japan.

SUSTAINABLE DEVELOPMENT

Japan's government is keen to promote sustainability. Laws have recently been introduced to require both the public and businesses to recycle. In 1997, it became illegal to dump electrical appliances, and in 2005, a similar law was passed to ensure that people dispose of their old cars in an environmentally responsible way. The management of waste in Japan poses a particular challenge, given the lack

▼ Car use has increased in Japan, with the number of registered cars on the road rising from 23 million in 1980 to more than 51 million in 2002.

of space and the high density of population in the country. Shortage of space for landfill sites has led to a reliance on incineration, with 78 percent of waste burned. However, public concern over dioxins, which can be released in the burning process, has made it increasingly difficult to build more incinerators.

While Japanese people are concerned about environmental issues, their concern does not always mean they voluntarily change their behavior. Some households, for example, still do not sort their waste into the different recycling containers provided by the authorities for different types of materials. Japan's government has begun to emphasize the importance of environmental education. Schools are encouraged to establish optional after-school clubs in which students can participate in conservation activities.

For Japan, many aspects of sustainability have an international dimension. For example, if fish stocks are to be protected, Japan needs to agree on sustainable practices with neighboring countries that share the stocks. In some cases, Japan has been accused of behaving in an unsustainable way in relation to other countries and shared environments. Its use of tropical hardwoods, for example, has contributed to deforestation in countries such as Malaysia, Papua New Guinea, Gabon, and Cameroon. But Japan has signed up to some international environmental agreements, including the international treaty tackling global warming and climate change, drawn up in Kyoto in 1997. In 1980, Japan also signed the Ramsar Convention, indicating a commitment to the protection of wetlands. Since signing, Japan has set aside eleven sites for protection, but most of them are small, some less than 250 acres (100 hectares), leaving much wetland habitat unprotected.

BIODIVERSITY AND CONSERVATION

The range of different habitats found in Japan allows for great biodiversity in the country. The

▲ In Tokyo, municipal waste is separated into different materials and collected on different days at designated collection points. This vehicle is collecting cardboard for recycling.

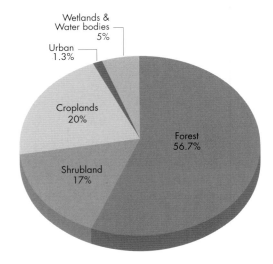

▲ Habitat type as percentage of total area

many smaller islands that are part of the country's archipelago are home to numerous species, including types of fungi and insects that are not found anywhere else in the world. Japan's "Green Census" is a national inventory that was established by the government in 1973. It lists and monitors details of the natural environment, including plants and animals, and is updated every five years. But while 25 percent of the country's land area is protected in some way, only 3 percent is protected specifically for nature conservation. Of Japan's animal and plant species, 20 percent, including golden eagles and Asiatic black bears, are threatened with extinction. This is because urbanization, intensive agriculture, forestry, and recreational activities and facilities have destroyed their habitats. Japan has tried to tackle issues of habitat protection and sustainability through initiatives such as the Basic Environment Law of 1993, which emphasizes the importance of the conservation of ecosystems.

Focus on: Japan and the International Ban on Commercial Whaling

Japan opposes the international ban on commercial whaling established by the International Whaling Commission (IWC) nearly twenty years ago. At a meeting of the IWC in 2005, Japan led a group of twenty-six nations, out of a total membership of sixty-two, in demanding an end to the ban (75 percent of countries needed to be in support for the ban to be overturned). Japan argues that fish stocks are threatened by an increasing whale population, that commercial whaling could take place without endangering whale species, and that some rural communities in Japan are suffering hardships because they cannot follow their traditional livelihood of whaling. The opinions of international scientific experts are divided on the whaling issue. Japan continues to hunt whales, killing more than 400 whales each year. It argues that these whales are killed for scientific purposes. Critics of Japan's position dispute this, partly because the whale meat is sold for people to eat. The eating of whale meat is generally accepted in Japan.

◀ Visitors look out over Ninety-Nine Islands National Park, which is located north of Nagasaki, on Kyushu. It is one of twenty-eight national parks in Japan.

Future Challenges

The recession of the 1990s has made Japan rethink some of its economic practices. In particular, the increasing industrial competition from countries such as South Korea and China has led Japanese companies to focus on the development of "one of a kind" high-tech products rather than mass produced goods. Political developments have also occurred. In 2001, Prime Minister Koizumi promised fundamental economic reforms, such as the privatization of the postal system, which would enable its fund of savings to be invested in private companies and not just state programs. Until 2005, progress towards these reforms was slower than promised because many politicians had gained from the state programs.

ENVIRONMENTAL PRESSURES

Although there has been increasing recognition in Japan that the environment is important,

pressures on it will continue. As the number of cars in Japan increases, air quality deteriorates, despite the fact that all vehicles in the country are now fitted with catalytic converters. Solutions to the waste-disposal problem are also urgently needed, and the government is emphasizing the importance of recycling. One challenge facing Japan's government is the need to protect the environment while still meeting the demands of consumers.

The government faces demands to protect the environment at a time when the economy is still recovering. Some environmental measures, such as greater energy conservation and the development of alternative energy sources to oil, could benefit the country's economy. Japan's continuing dependence on oil imports is clearly a problem, in spite of the fact that it has been reduced from the level of the 1970s. Also,

◀ Two Japanese red-crested cranes perform a territorial dance in the winter snows of Hokkaido. The protection of endangered species such as red-crested cranes is a considerable challenge for Japan in the future.

nuclear power is no longer the obvious solution to the energy crisis, as its dangers have been highlighted by recent accidents at nuclear reactors. Further questions about nuclear waste disposal have led to increased public concern.

POPULATION CHANGES

Some see the increasing age of Japan's population as the greatest challenge the country faces. These people predict a health and pension system under strain and a crisis in the care of the elderly. Traditionally, female family members have cared for the elderly, but with more women working outside the home, this way of life is being eroded. Increased numbers of women in the workforce also contributed to the decrease in young people in Japan because working women have fewer babies. One way out of this problem might be for older people to keep working. In a prosperous country like Japan, the elderly remain healthy far longer than in the past, so they may be encouraged to continue in productive employment.

JAPAN IN THE WORLD

For the past sixty years, Japan's foreign policy has been based on the part of its constitution that forbids the use of military means to deal with international disputes. Over the past few years, however, Japan has given signs that it is questioning this principle. In particular, Japan feels threatened by North Korea's military policies and, because of this, is starting to look at building up its own military with a missile defense system bought from the United States. As a result of this regional tension, Japan is likely to maintain, and even strengthen, its ties with the United States.

Japan's position as the most economically powerful nation in the East Asian region is increasingly challenged by rapid development in China. At present, China is Japan's biggest trading partner. It remains to be seen whether the two countries can build a cooperative partnership that is based on their existing strong trade links. If their rivalry intensifies, the stability and security of the region might be threatened.

▲ The new Fuji Television headquarters in Tokyo was designed by Tange Kenzo, a famous Japanese architect. The building is an example of Japan's continuing modernization and innovation.

Time Line

300 B.C.–A.D. 300 During the Yayoi Era, ideas brought by migrants from China strongly influence Japanese society.

1192 Minamoto Yoritomo becomes the first ruling shogun.

1549 Christianity is introduced to Japan by Jesuit missionary Francis Xavier.

1707 The last recorded eruption of Mount Fuji.

1871 The feudal system is abolished.

1872 Baseball is introduced to Japan.

1889 An Imperial Household Law is passed forbidding women from ascending to the Chrysanthemum Throne.

1914–1918 Japan fights on the side of the Allies in World War I.

1923 The Great Kanto earthquake devastates the Tokyo area.

1937 War between China and Japan escalates and later becomes part of World War II.

1941 Japan launches an attack on the U.S. Navy base at Pearl Harbor; the United States responds by declaring war on Japan.

1945 Atomic bombs are dropped on Hiroshima and Nagasaki by the United States military.

1947 A new constitution, written by the U.S. occupying power, is established in Japan. Women are allowed to vote.

1964 The first section of high-speed rail track for the bullet trains opens.

1993 The Liberal Democratic Party, which had been the ruling political party in Japan since the 1950s, loses power.

1998 Japan hosts the Winter Olympics.

2001 The Liberal Democratic Party is returned to power, and Junichiro Koizumi becomes prime minister.

2002 Japan and South Korea co-host the soccer World Cup.

2005 Anti-Japanese protests in China and South Korea are sparked by the publication in Japan of a history textbook that omits mention of Japan's wartime atrocities.

2005 The Liberal Democratic Party wins a general election with the biggest majority in twenty years.

Glossary

Allies (World War I) the countries, including France, Russia, Britain, Italy, and the United States, that fought against Germany in World War I

Allies (World War II) the countries, including France, Britain, Canada, and the United States, that fought against Germany, Italy, and Japan in World War II

analog having to do with technology that uses electrical waves to transmit information

annex to take possession of a country or an area of land, usually by force or without permission

annexation the taking possession of a country by another country

Asian Tigers the Asian countries, including South

Korea, Taiwan, Singapore, Hong Kong, and China, that achieved high economic growth by producing large quantities of goods for sale abroad

coalition the union of different political parties or groups for a particular purpose, usually for a limited time period

communist someone who believes in an economic system that abolishes private ownership and emphasizes common ownership of means of production and government control

constitution a written document that sets out the political principles by which a nation is governed

democratic having to do with a system of government based on the principle that all adult citizens should be allowed to vote for people to represent them in government

digital having to do with technology that converts information into a code and transmits it quickly

dioxins poisonous chemicals that are released when certain substances, such as plastics, are burned

Dutch East India Company a trade organization established in the Netherlands in 1602 to carry out foreign trading, particularly with the Dutch colonies but also with independent countries such as Japan

Edo era an era of Japanese history named after the capital city of the time; Edo is now renamed Tokyo

expansionism the act of increasing the amount of land ruled over by a country, often by force

G8 a group of the eight leading industrialized countries in the world; the G8 meets every year to discuss issues of global importance, such as the fight against AIDS

geothermal having to do with heat inside Earth

greenhouse gas emissions gases, released into Earth's atmosphere by human activity and natural processes that absorb and trap heat from the sun in the planet's atmosphere; these emissions include carbon dioxide, methane, and nitrous oxides

hereditary having to do with processes by which properties are passed from parent to child

hierarchy a system in which people are ranked according to their importance

homogenous similar or of the same type

indigenous original or native to an area or country

Manchuria an area of approximately 77,220 sq miles (200,000 sq km) in the northeast of Asia that lies within the borders of China

nationalism loyalty or devotion to one's country, which, in extreme forms, includes the belief that one's country is better than all others

pentatonic scale a musical scale that is made up of five notes

precipitation water falling from clouds, usually in the form of rain or snow

prefectures political districts of Japan that are like states or counties

representative government a government that speaks for a group of people who have had some influence in choosing its members

SARS (Severe Acute Respiratory Syndrome) a dangerous form of pneumonia that first appeared in China in 2002

seismically having to do with or caused by earthquakes

shogun a ruler of Japan between 1192 and 1868

sustainability a way of life and a means of economic development that can be continued at the same level into the future without damaging the environment

tectonic plates the large rigid blocks that make up the surface of Earth's crust

tsunami a giant sea surge affecting coastal areas that is triggered by movements of Earth's crust or volcanic eruptions under the sea

Yayoi era an era of Japanese history named after the area of Tokyo in which archaeological investigations uncovered the first recognized traces of its history

United Nations (UN) an international organization established after World War II in 1945 with the goal of maintaining international peace and security and promoting international economic and social cooperation

UN Security Council a part of the UN that focuses on maintaining peace between nations

Further Information

BOOKS TO READ

Barber, Nicola. *Tokyo* (Great Cities of the World). World Almanac Library, 2004.

Dowswell, Paul. *Pearl Harbor* (Days that Shook the World). Hodder Wayland, 2002.

Ganeri, Anita. *Buddhism* (Religions of the World). World Almanac Library, 2006.

Green, Jen. *Japan* (Nations of the World). Raintree, 2004.

Guile, M. *Japan* (Culture in . . .). Heinemann, 2003).

Hook, Jason. *Hiroshima* (Days that Shook the World). Hodder Wayland, 2003.

Lansford, L., and C. Scharz. *Japan* (Changing Face of . . .). Hodder Wayland, 2004.

Okum, D. *Manga Madness*. North Light Books, 2004.

Whyte, Harlinah. *Japan* (Countries of the World). Gareth Stevens, 1998.

USEFUL WEB SITES

The Ainu Museum
www.ainu-museum.or.jp/english/english.html

CIA World Factbook: Japan
www.odci.gov/cia/publications/factbook/

The Economist: Japan
www.economist.com/countries/Japan

Edo Japan: A Virtual Tour
http://www.us-japan.org/edomatsu/

Library of Congress Country Study: Japan
http://lcweb2.loc.gov/frd/cs/jptoc.html

NOVA: Japan's Secret Garden
http://www.pbs.org/wgbh/nova/satoyama/

Web Japan: Gateway for All Japanese Information
http://web-japan.org/index.html

About the Author

Celia Tidmarsh is a geography PGCE tutor at the Graduate School of Education, University of Bristol. She has taught geography in secondary schools in Britain for fifteen years.

She has written geography text books for young people on various topics and has also carried out research on children's attitudes toward nature and environmental issues.

FREE PUBLIC LIBRARY UNION, NEW JERSEY

3 9549 00379 6050